4/07

KIDS &
COMPUTERS

W9-CQB-392

JURTBERG

Kids & Computers

The Supercomputers

Charles A. Jortberg

Published by Abdo & Daughters, 4940 Viking Drive, Suite 622, Edina, Minnesota 55435.

Copyright © 1997 by Abdo Consulting Group, Inc., Pentagon Tower, P.O. Box 36036, Minneapolis, Minnesota 55435 USA. International copyrights reserved in all countries. No part of this book may be reproduced in any form without written permission from the publisher.

Printed in the United States.

Cover and Interior Photo credits: Wide World Photos
Archive Photos
Jortberg Associates

Edited by John Hamilton

Library of Congress Cataloging-in-Publication Data

Jortberg, Charles A.
The supercomputers / Charles A. Jortberg.
    p. cm. -- (Kids and computers)
Includes index.
Summary: Describes the development and past and present uses of some of the most powerful computers ever designed.
ISBN 1-56239-724-9
1. Supercomputers--Juvenile literature. [1. Supercomputers. 2. Computers.] I. Title. II. Series: Jortberg, Charles A.   Kids and computers.
QA76.88.J67   1997
004.1'2'09--DC20   96-28294
                                                                          CIP
                                                                          AC

About the Author

Charles A. Jortberg graduated from Bowdoin College in 1951 with a Bachelor's Degree in Economics. Mr. Jortberg joined IBM in 1954 and served in several capacities. Among his assignments were coordinating all of IBM's efforts with the Air Force, managing a 20-person team of IBM engineers, and directing a number of technical programs at NASA's Electronic Research Laboratory. He formed Jortberg Associates in 1972, where he currently works, to provide an outlet for his start up technology experience.

Contents

UNIVAC

After designing the big computer systems for the U.S. government, scientists soon set their sights on producing computers for use in business. This began a period of amazing expansion in the number and quality of large computer systems.

When John Eckert and John Mauchly formed the Eckert-Mauchly Computer Corporation, they designed a big machine called the UNIVAC, which included many of the ideas from their work at the University of Pennsylvania. Finding themselves without the money to finish the UNIVAC machine, they sold their company to Remington Rand, a company that sold punched card systems similar to IBM's. The first UNIVAC was installed at the U.S. Census Bureau—where Herman Hollerith had invented the punched card.

The UNIVAC attracted national attention because it was the first computer to count returns in a national election. In 1952, in front of a national TV audience, the machine predicted that Eisenhower would win over Adlai Stevenson, only 45 minutes after the polls closed. This was a very exciting development, since most people had never even heard of a computer. The bright lights and whirring magnetic tapes created a picture that to many people resembled science fiction. For many years the term UNIVAC was used to describe any computer.

The UNIVAC was followed by other machines from IBM, Burroughs, and the National Cash Register Company. All of these machines were very large. They needed special rooms built for them because they needed to be air conditioned all the time. The rooms had false floors, built so that the computers could sit about one foot above the regular floor. These false floors were needed so that the big cables that connected the machines could be strung out under the floor. Otherwise, people would trip over them.

The UNIVAC machine in 1955.

NASA and Big Business

The big machines were used to solve many problems. For years there were computers that were better for the sciences, and others that were better for business problems. In the sciences, big machines solved many complex problems, such as those faced by NASA. When the manned space flights were planned, these big machines did all the calculating needed to design the rockets, the spacecraft, and the orbits that would be flown, and where and how the craft would return to earth.

The big business computers were run by large banks, insurance companies, and several government agencies. The banks were among the earliest users of the big machines. In addition to keeping track of millions of accounts, they also had to process millions of checks each day.

New check-sorting machines were invented that were similar to some of the early punched card sorters. All of the banks got together and agreed on a special code that could be printed on checks, where the account number was printed on the bottom of the check. If you look at a check today you will see the numbers printed on the bottom. The odd-looking square-type numbers are printed that way so that the bank sorters can read the account numbers.

NASA's top administrators get a firsthand look at the Cray-2 supercomputer.

The SABRE System

Other users of these giant computer systems were the airlines and railroads. The computers were just the answer for the problem of making reservations for customers and checking to be sure there was space available before tickets were sold. The biggest of these systems was built for American Airlines by IBM. The system was known as the SABRE system. Even though it first started to handle reservations in 1964, it is still operating today. Over the years the big computers in the system have been changed to make them bigger and faster. The computers use huge disk memories to keep track of every seat on every flight for months ahead of time.

The computer in these systems first used a kind of typewriter called a "Teletype" connected to the computer by telephone lines from all over the country. Most teletypes have since been replaced with display units. In most locations personal computers are used to communicate with the gigantic memory. These terminals are located in every travel agent's office. If you do a lot of traveling you can even make your own reservations from your computer.

American Airlines ticket processor using the SABRE system developed by IBM.

The heaviest users of big computers from the U.S. government included the Census Bureau and the U.S. Post Office. The biggest government user is still the Social Security Administration, which keeps salary records of every wage earner in the country. Another early government user was the Internal Revenue Service. This agency keeps track of all the taxpayers in the United States, as well as every business. Every dollar paid in taxes is processed by one of these huge systems.

Soon there were eight big companies selling big computers in the United States. IBM and Sperry Rand were joined by Burroughs, National Cash Register, Control Data Corporation, RCA, Honeywell, and General Electric. For many years when people talked about the computer business they referred to "Snow White and the Seven Dwarfs." IBM was Snow White and the other seven companies were the dwarfs. Of these companies, a number of them have stopped making computers, including General Electric, RCA, Honeywell, and Control Data. Burroughs and Sperry Rand joined together to become Unisys.

Programming Systems

With the growth in the number of big computers also came several developments in preparing the machines to solve problems. These new ideas were needed if the use of computers was to expand as fast as the engineers could design them. When the first computers were built, the instructions to run them had to be wired into the machines by hand. The punched card computers were equipped with control panels for each problem. Any time you wanted to solve another problem you had to wire another control panel and put it in the machine.

In the ENIAC computer, the instructions were wired into the machine with long cables. For each problem to be solved the wires had to be pulled out and reset. All the computers required instructions for every single thing to be done. These instructions then had to be entered into the machine. The preparation of these instructions was called "programming."

These machines are really not smart and do only what they are instructed to perform. This early programming work was very hard, and each problem could take weeks to program. The program steps for the SAGE computer, when punched into cards, could reach over 33 miles if the cards were laid end to end.

Once the instructions were written down, they were entered into the computer memory. This was usually done by keyboard, or the instructions were punched into cards, which were then read into the computer. Most of these early program steps were written as a series of 1's and 0's, which the computer then changed to electrical signals. It was easy to make mistakes when thousands of these numbers had to be entered.

There were several efforts to improve the writing of programs and to make it easier to get the computers to solve problems. Among the first solutions was a system developed at Dartmouth College in New Hampshire. Through the efforts of Professor John Kemeny, a new programming system called "BASIC" was developed. In BASIC the programmer used a form of English abbreviations to instruct the computer what to do. For every English instruction, the BASIC system would convert it to the necessary 1's and 0's. The increase in speed in writing programs was better than anyone expected. Soon every computer company was using some form of BASIC.

Dr. John Kemeny, developer of the BASIC programming system.

The Mark I Computer

Grace Hopper, an officer in the U.S. Navy, soon changed the way programs were written—and greatly eased the problem of writing programs for business computers.

Hopper enlisted in the Navy in 1943, leaving a teaching assignment at Barnard College. She became an officer and was assigned to the Navy project at Harvard University, where Howard Aiken was working on the Mark I computer. This computer was being used to trace the path of shells from guns aboard ships. While serving at Harvard, Hopper learned how hard it was to change all the wires every time you wanted to solve a new problem. She vowed that someday she would find a better way to enter programs.

During the time Hopper was at Harvard, the computer stopped one morning and no one knew why. Eventually, the scientists found a moth stuck in one of the big switches in the machine. This was the first use of the term "debug."

After the war, Hopper worked for Remington Rand, which became Sperry Rand in 1953. There she wrote several papers explaining her ideas on how computers could help write their own programs. Her ideas included the concept of writing instructions for the computer in English and having the computer itself produce all the 0's and 1's it needed. This computer program became known as a "compiler."

With Hopper's basic ideas, compilers have been used over the past several years. A special compiler for scientific work is called FORTRAN. This stands for FORmula TRANslation. With Fortran you wrote out the

Grace Hopper at work on a manual tape punch machine.

mathematical steps needed to solve a problem. If you wanted to multiply a number called "A" times a number called "B," all you had to do was write the letters A*B, where the "*" means multiply. The compiler produced all of the 0's and 1's the computer needed. For every program step you wrote, the compiler produced several steps the machine would need.

The time saving was terrific. Programs that before needed weeks to complete were now done in hours. Grace Hopper returned to the Navy in 1967 and served in several important jobs dealing with computers. She became a Rear Admiral before she retired.

IBM's Efforts

During the time that the UNIVAC was getting so much attention, IBM was busy finishing the design of a big computer called the IBM Electronic Data Processing Machine. When this machine was announced it was known as the IBM 701 Computer. Each one of these machines cost $17,000 each month to own. It is hard to realize that for this amount of money you got a machine that was much slower than today's personal computers, which you can buy for around $1,500.

At first IBM wasn't in a big hurry to make computers. Some in the company didn't think there was much of a future for stored-program machines. But when they saw all the attention that UNIVAC was getting, they changed their mind quickly and began a crash program to catch up. The IBM 701 was quickly followed by a series of big machines for business and science.

Computer scientists were creating new ideas so fast that new designs were in use for only five years before they were replaced by better machines. Every group of new computers in the last 40 years has more than doubled in speed, and yet prices have continued to drop. New inventions in electronics have allowed this to happen.

Timesharing

One of the important developments with the big machines was called "timesharing." At the Massachusetts Institute of Technology (MIT) in Cambridge, Massachusetts, a large computer was installed for research projects and to teach students about computers. But there were thousands of students

IBM data processing system.

and only one large machine. Professors Robert Fano and Fernando Corbat wondered how to make the machines available to a number of students. They decided to connect the machines by wires and telephone lines.

A student operates a terminal which is part of a larger computer system.

At each location the students had a station resembling a typewriter. The student typed in a problem and the computer calculated the answer and sent it back to the remote location over the cable or telephone line. Because the computer was so fast, each student had the impression it was working only on his or her problem. The computer was actually working on several problems at once, and thus was "timesharing."

This program allowed MIT to expose many students to the use of computers and to develop a familiarity with the machines. This allowed these students the chance to work on new programs for the growth of other computer applications. Dartmouth College in New Hampshire also offered the same type of program. This type of program is not needed much any more, because most students now have their own personal computers.

Other Advances

As the developments of new computers progressed quickly, so did the changes in the devices used with these machines. Printers on the first big machines worked at only 150 lines per minute. New printer developments allowed printed reports at over 10,000 lines per minute. The use of lasers allowed this great increase in speed.

With this type of printer, a laser beam is guided by the computer to trace written characters on a drum that is coated with a special material. Where the laser beams strikes the drum it produces small electrical charges. These charges act like a magnet, attracting a black powder called toner. When the drum turns, the toner is transferred to the paper. The paper is then heated to make the toner stick to the paper better. This type of laser printing is now commonly used in all copiers, and also on many small printers used with personal computers.

An IBM technician examines a new laser printer.

Magnetic Tape

The use of small magnetic tape cassettes expanded so much, for years tape was the main method of storing information outside the computer. Some of the early tapes were made of metal, and a reel weighed over 50 pounds. They were much too heavy for the average person to take on and off. It wasn't long before all tapes were made of Mylar, a commonly available plastic.

In 1956, information was recorded on magnetic tape with 100 numbers or letters recorded on every inch. The tape could pass through the machine at the rate of 75 inches per second, so the machine could read 100 x 75, or 7,500 characters every second. It wasn't long before tapes were moving at 200 inches per second, with the tape storing 6,250 numbers or letters in every inch. These later tape units were reading or writing at 1.25 million characters each second.

**View of a data processing room showing
magnetic tape units.**

Magnetic Disks

It was in this era that the first disk drives also appeared. In 1956 IBM announced a machine called the 305 RAMAC, which had a revolutionary type of external memory. The memory consisted of 50 big disks that revolved at high speed. Each of these disks was coated with the same material as magnetic tape. This group of disks could store 15 million letters or numbers. While the disks were spinning, an arm moved in and out with a special reading head that sensed the stored information and transferred it in and out of the computer. The heads were designed to actually fly over the disk surface. They were shaped like the wing of an airplane and came within thousandths of an inch of the disk without touching it. Sometimes, just like a plane, the heads crashed. When this happened, the head would land on the disk and gouge it, destroying data.

The disk unit was very big, almost reaching the ceiling. The concept of disk memory soon became very popular. When you need an item of information, the arm and reading head go right to the place on the disk where the information is stored. If you have information on the end of a tape reel, you have to search the entire reel before you get to it.

The capacities of disks continued to increase. Today, their cost and size has decreased so much that the small 3.5-inch disks now used on personal computers can store more than two million numbers or letters.

National Cash Register Company built a different system of large storage called a Card Random Access Machine. They called it a CRAM. It was a big round tub with hundreds of punched cards hanging by notches on rods. When the computer needed a card, a gripper found the right card, wrapped it around a drum, and the information was then read. The card was then gripped again and put back on the rods in the tub. The U.S. Air Force made very good use of the CRAM file in its computers.

The 305 RAMAC was one of the first computers to use external disk memory.

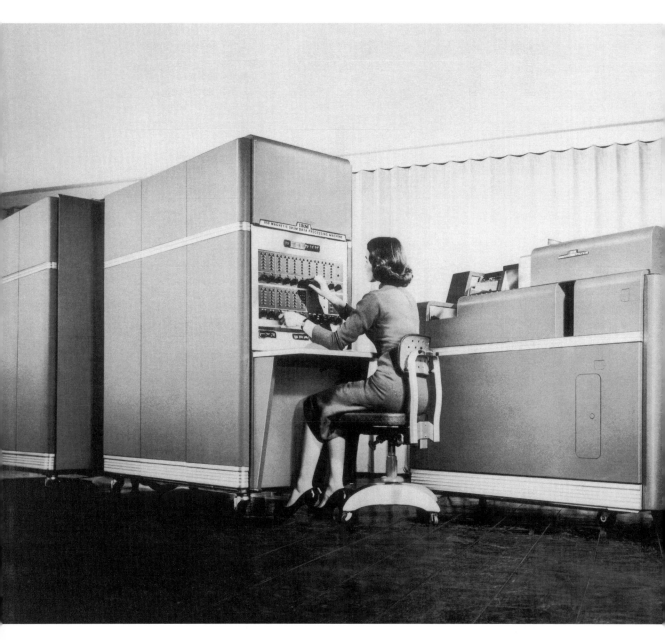

IBM 650 magnetic drum data processing machine.

The Smaller Machines

Because there were only a few companies that could afford the huge, expensive machines, computer companies started to design smaller, less expensive units that could be used by more people. Among the most popular was a machine known as the IBM 650. This machine used a different form of memory called a magnetic drum. This drum was a steel cylinder coated with the same material used to make magnetic tape. By magnetizing parts of the drum, the 1's and 0's representing numbers and letters could be stored. To prove how reliable this memory was, IBM engineers took a magnetic drum off a computer in New York, placed it on an open truck, and then drove to California. They then placed the drum on another computer and found they hadn't lost a single number or letter.

The Mini-computer

In the early 1960s many people in IBM and other companies didn't believe that there would ever be a use for smaller machines. It turned out, however, that they were very wrong. A company in Massachusetts called Digital Equipment Corporation (DEC) was started by people who had worked at MIT on some of the early big machines. DEC designed a small computer that was the size of a desk, instead of the room-sized giants that were being used in many places. Because of its smaller size, the machine was called a "minicomputer."

Minicomputers were different in a number of ways from the older machines. Instead of needing a large group of engineers to get them working, they were delivered in a box and set up by the buyer. These machines didn't need special air conditioning or big rooms with lots of cables connecting all of the parts of the computer. They were smaller than the older machines in the types of problems they could solve, since they didn't have the big magnetic tape units, printers, or memories.

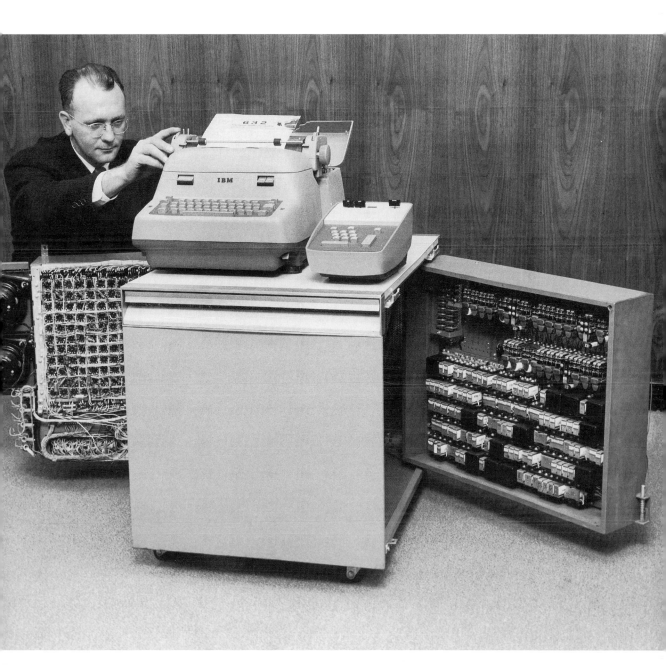

The 632 was IBM's first minicomputer.

Although the new computers were smaller, this didn't mean they weren't powerful. There were many technical problems and scientific experiments that could be done as well, if not better, with these machines. Minicomputers were built so that scientific instruments could be directly attached to them, without the need for creating punched cards or some other means of entering data.

In addition to the machines from DEC, one of the earliest computers for scientific use was the LINC computer. This name came from the first letters of the long name of the computer, the Laboratory Instrument Computer. The LINC, designed by Wes Clark, allowed scientists to design experiments with the computer directly connected to patients in hospitals, or to animals used in laboratory tests. At one time the LINC was directly attached to a cat's brain so that doctors could study the electrical patterns. The LINC was installed in many hospitals to assist them in medical experiments.

The minicomputer opened up several areas of computer use that had not been thought of before. Among these was the introduction of the computer into the business office, so that secretaries could use them for writing letters and keeping track of documents. This became known as "word processing," and quickly became the most common use of these smaller computers. This growth was due largely to the ideas of Dr. An Wang.

The Wangwriter

Dr. Wang came to the United States from China to become an electrical engineer. He invented many parts still used in computers today, and also designed a new electric calculator that was sold by a company he started. This company was named Wang Laboratories. Dr. Wang saw that word processing could be a wonderful use of a computer because of the thousands of offices with people writing millions of lines in letters and reports.

Wang Laboratories started selling small computer systems designed to do only word processing. These machines were very inexpensive, costing much less than many of the minicomputers that were sold for other uses. The number of these machines that were sold surprised even Dr. Wang. Thousands of these computers were installed in every type of location.

Dr. Wang with his Wangwriter.

The Wang word processing computer was small, taking up the space of a normal desk. It was equipped with a keyboard, a small processor, a typewriter-like printer, a TV-type screen, and a disk unit that used a small floppy disk. Using this machine, called a "Wangwriter," you could write a report using the keyboard. When you hit a key the letter or number appeared on the screen and was stored in the machine's memory. Once you had finished your document, you would then hit a button and the machine would print the report.

After you were finished, the report could then be recorded on magnetic disk. Anytime later, if you wanted to read the report again or change it, all you had to do was to put the disk back in the computer and you could look at it again. The machine would also allow you to enter new words in the middle of sentences or erase words, sentences, or complete paragraphs. All these things became known as "editing." Other things you could do included having the computer check the spelling.

Wang then built a larger version of the Wangwriter and set it up so that several people could use the computer at the same time. Each of these users would sit at their desk with a keyboard and a TV-type screen. These were connected to the computer by a cable that was usually hidden in the wall. Because the computer had a big memory and was faster than the Wangwriter, it could handle a number of users at the same time.

There were many new uses of the minicomputers, as people began to realize that they didn't have to buy one of the giant machines in order to gain the benefits of the stored program. Medical laboratories used them to record the results of blood and other tests, operating rooms in hospitals used them to keep close attention to patients, and special machines built to do detailed cutting of metal parts were driven by minicomputers.

Glossary

application software - programs designed to perform specific tasks, such as games, educational programs, or payroll programs.

BASIC - Beginner's All-purpose Symbolic Instruction Code. A computer language designed for beginners.

cassette - two miniature tape reels contained in a plastic housing.

compact disk (CD) - a large volume of permenantly stored data formed by burning small holes in the surface with a laser.

compiler - a program designed to translate a high-level language into machine language prior to the execution of a program.

debug - to fix a computer.

disk - a flat, rotating circular sheet used to store bits of information.

display unit - a television receiver used to display computer output.

external memory - memory located outside the computer.

floppy disk - a small magnetic disk used to transfer information to and from a computer.

FORTRAN - FORmula TRANslator - a language used to write programs for mathematical problems.

hard disk drive - an internal disk memory that consists of disks which store millions of bits of data.

keyboard - an input device, normally comprising a standard set of keys like that on a typewriter.

laser - a device that produces an extremely powerful beam of light.

magnetic tape - tape that stores data in the form of magnetic impulses.

minicomputer - a small computer based on large computer technology.

modem - a communications device that enables a computer to transmit information over a standard telephone line.

mouse - a device that enables people to communicate with their computers. It is used to move the cursor to any point on the screen of a computer display

mylar - a special plastic used to make magnetic tape.

NASA - National Aeronautics and Space Administration. A U. S. government agency that oversees the country's space program.

personal computer (PC) - a small, powerful general-use computer.

program - an organized group of instructions that tells the computer what to do.

punched card system - a way of programming a computer using a series of punched cards.

stored program - a program that is stored inside the computer.

supercomputer - a powerful computer that operates at a high rate of speed.

terminal - a keyboard and display unit used for input and output.

timesharing - an arrangement where a central processing system serves several users over telephone lines.

word processing - a special application of a computer in which the user manipulates text.

Index